A Story About Laura

by Licia Martinucci-Marsh • illustrated by Craig Spearing

SCHOLASTIC INC.
New York   Toronto   London   Auckland   Sydney
Mexico City   New Delhi   Hong Kong   Buenos Aires

No part of this publication may be reproduced in whole or in part, or stored in a retrieval system, or transmitted in any form or by any means, electronic, mechanical, photocopying, recording, or otherwise, without written permission of the publisher. For information regarding permission, write to Scholastic Inc., Education Group, 555 Broadway, New York, NY 10012.

Developed by Kirchoff/Wohlberg, Inc., in cooperation with Scholastic Inc.

Copyright © 2002 by Scholastic Inc.
All rights reserved.   Published by Scholastic Inc.   Printed in the U.S.A.
ISBN 0-439-35118-9
SCHOLASTIC and associated logos and designs are trademarks
and/or registered trademarks of Scholastic Inc.
5 6 7 8 9 10   23   09 08 07 06 05

In the late 1860s, many people traveled across America to the West. They wanted a better life. Families collected everything they had. They loaded up covered wagons. The wagons had canvas covers for protection against rain, sun, and wind. The loaded wagon lurched forward, pulled by a team of horses. It took a very long time to travel in those days.

Laura Ingalls was one of those pioneers. We know about what their life was like because of Laura's stories.

Laura wrote about life in the big woods during the pioneer days. She was born on February 7, 1867, near Pepin, Wisconsin. The next year, her Ma and Pa moved Laura and her older sister, Mary, to Missouri. They didn't stay there for long. In fact, the Ingalls family moved many times while Laura was little.

At that time, settlers could get land from the government. They could get it for free if they farmed it and lived on it for five years. Pa decided to settle on some land in Kansas. He built a house and stable with the help of a neighbor.

The family planted crops and a prairie garden. Another daughter, Carrie, was born. Not long after, though, the family was forced to leave. Their land was the home of Native Americans. The government decided to take the land back from the settlers. The Ingalls hitched up their wagon and moved back to the big woods of Wisconsin. Three years later, in 1874, they moved to a place called Plum Creek, near Walnut Grove, Minnesota.

Pa built a new house there. The family worked hard to plant more crops.

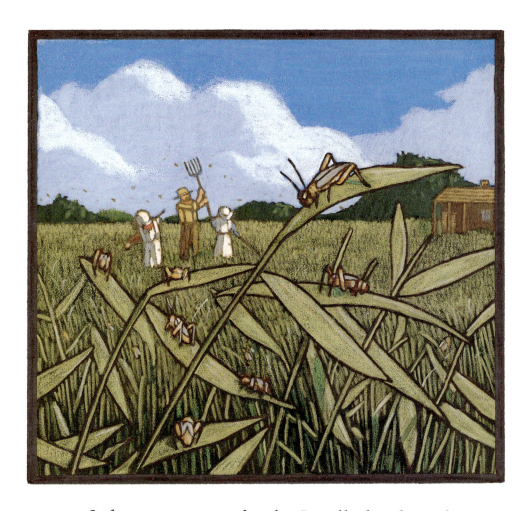

   Life was not easy for the Ingalls family and other settlers. They often faced hard weather and other trouble. The winters were freezing cold. One time, they had so much snow that trains could not carry supplies to the settlers. Many people did not get enough to eat.
   In 1874, thousands of grasshoppers swept over the land. They ate the wheat crops, vegetables, and even clothing. Many settlers left their land because of this disaster.

The Ingalls left Minnesota and moved to Dakota Territory. They were among the first settlers to arrive there. For the second time, the Ingalls family owned a farm. Once again they planted crops and a garden.

Laura helped Ma cook. Laura also liked to sew. She learned how to make clothes and mend things. Even though life was hard for the Ingalls, they were a happy and close family.

The family did many things together. They read books aloud to each other. They sang songs. Laura especially loved when Pa played his fiddle.

He played very well and always had a pretty melody ready. When he played, Laura would dance with her sisters while Ma kept time.

Pa would also tell stories. Laura and her sisters listened to every word. Sometimes he spoke of his childhood. Sometimes he told the girls about cowboys and their adventures.

In 1876, the Ingalls family moved again to Burr Oak, Iowa. Their friends, the Steadmans, owned a hotel there. They asked Pa to help them, but he did not like running a hotel. The family got homesick for Walnut Grove. They returned there in 1877.

Two years later, Laura's older sister Mary became very sick. She lost her sight. To help Mary, Laura described what she saw. Laura talked about the colors of a sunset or the way the leaves changed in the fall. Mary said that Laura was very good at this. "You make pictures when you talk, Laura," she said.

Later that year, the Ingalls moved one last time back to Dakota Territory. By this time, Laura was a teenager. She had become very shy. She had a hard time making friends. Still, she worked very hard at her schoolwork. She got good grades in English, history, and poetry.

When she was 15, Laura became a teacher. She was very young to have a job. She worked so her sister, Mary, could attend a special school for the blind.

The school was 12 miles away from Laura's home. That was very far in those days. She had to live with a family who lived near the school. Laura was very lonely. She missed her family. A nice young man named Almanzo Wilder offered to drive her home each weekend so that she could visit. She and Almanzo became good friends. Three years later, in 1885, they got married. A year later, their daughter, Rose, was born. The new family was happy, but life was still very hard.

More bad weather came. There were droughts and hailstorms. They lost their crops. They had very little money. Almanzo became sick and could not work for a while. Things got worse when their house burned down a year later. No matter what happened to them, Laura and Almanzo always managed to get through it somehow.

The Wilders finally settled in Missouri. They bought a house and some land and named it Rocky Ridge Farm. The house was a small log cabin. Over many years, Laura and Almanzo added to the little house. It became a large farmhouse. They had 200 acres of land and a herd of cows. They had pigs and hens too. Laura and Almanzo did all of this work by themselves. When they had free time, they rode horses, told stories, or played music.

Laura started to write for a farming newspaper. Her first article was published in 1911. Soon she was writing for other publishers. She enjoyed writing. Many people enjoyed reading her articles too.

Laura wrote her first novel when she was in her sixties. Most people stop working at this age. Laura's daughter, Rose, had asked her many times to write about her childhood. Rose thought that other children might like to read about Laura's life as a frontier girl.

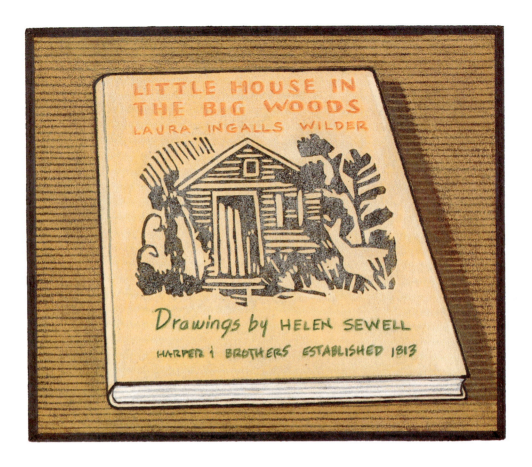

    Rose was right. Laura's first novel was called "Little House in the Big Woods." It was published in 1932. Children all over the world loved it. They wrote Laura many letters asking her to write more books. Laura Ingalls Wilder wrote a total of nine books. She won many awards for them.

    Laura was the first person to win an award for children's books. One award is even named for her. The Laura Ingalls Wilder Medal is still given every three years to honor someone for writing good children's books.

Laura's husband, Almanzo, died on October 23, 1949. He was 92 years old. He and Laura had been married for 63 years. Laura Ingalls Wilder died on February 10, 1957, at her Rocky Ridge Farm. She was 90 years old.

Even today, children love to read Laura's books, just as they did years ago. Her books tell us about things that will always be important.

Many of the lessons Laura teaches us are true today. It is best to be honest and to make the most of what we have. We must always try to be happy with simple things. We must never give up when things go wrong.

Laura Ingalls Wilder was a true pioneer girl. Because of the wonderful books she wrote, we will always know what pioneer life was like.